FATAL OBSESSIONS

Fatal Obsessions

A Journey into the Minds of Serial Killers

MORGAN JEFFERY

Better than Bonkers

Contents

Chapter 1

Introduction to Serial Killers

The Definition and History of Serial Killers

The phenomenon of serial killers has perpetually captivated and unsettled society, engendering a macabre curiosity that propels true crime enthusiasts and criminology students into the labyrinthine recesses of their distorted minds. This subchapter endeavors to provide an exhaustive understanding of the definition and historical evolution of serial killers, tailored to the nuanced interests of various subcultures. These include enthusiasts intrigued by female serial killers, those engrossed in unsolved serial killings, individuals fascinated by specific modus operandi, and those intrigued by killers targeting distinct demographics or operating within particular regions or countries. Furthermore, we will traverse the mysterious realm of serial killers who evaded capture, leaving behind an unresolved tapestry of questions and horrors.

Commencing with the paramount task of establishing a crystalline definition of a serial killer, we recognize these individuals as those who, over a protracted period, commit a series of murders with distinctive intervals between each crime—a pattern setting them apart from other types of murderers. The historical odyssey of serial killers reveals their existence throughout the annals of time, donned in different guises. From ancient times with enigmatic figures like Gilles de Rais and Elizabeth Bathory to the infamous 20th-century culprits such as Ted Bundy and John Wayne Gacy, this subchapter embarks on a riveting journey, tracing the metamorphosis of serial killers and their evolving methods.

For avid true crime enthusiasts, the subchapter intricately explores specific niches that have ensnared their attention. Unveiling the chilling world of female serial killers—a lesser-known yet equally unsettling subgroup—it sheds light on their motivations and the distinctive elements characterizing their crimes. Unsolved serial killings, exemplified by the enigmatic Zodiac Killer case, are scrutinized, unraveling the enduring mysteries that continue to captivate investigators and armchair detectives alike.

Venturing into the modus operandi of serial killers,

the subchapter delves into various methods employed, including strangulation, poisoning, and other specific techniques that distinguish them. Additionally, it meticulously examines cases where serial killers selectively targeted certain demographics, such as children or prostitutes, offering insights into the unsettling motivations behind these choices.

Furthermore, the geographical facet of serial killings is laid bare, dissecting infamous cases from specific regions or countries and spotlighting the cultural and societal factors that may have contributed to these heinous crimes.

Concluding this comprehensive exploration, the subchapter immerses readers in the enigmatic realm of unsolved cases, where serial killers cunningly evaded capture, leaving behind a legacy of unanswered questions and unresolved horrors. Woven seamlessly throughout are the psychological profiles of serial killers, drawing from the realms of psychology, criminology, and forensic science. This exploration unravels the intricate factors contributing to their homicidal tendencies, such as childhood trauma, psychopathy, or a chilling desire for power and control.

In summary, "The Definition and History of Serial Killers" subchapter is an intricate tapestry that weaves together the dark and twisted world of serial killers. Tailored for true crime enthusiasts, criminology students, and diverse niche audiences, it not only provides a deeper understanding of this phenomenon but also casts an illuminating spotlight on the motivations, methods, and psychological profiles that shape the minds of these chilling individuals.

The Fascination with Serial Killers in Popular Culture

The enigmatic allure of serial killers has entrenched itself deeply within the folds of popular culture, captivating the morbid fascination of true crime enthusiasts and criminology students alike. The shocking and heinous crimes committed by these individuals have transcended mere headlines, evolving into a pervasive mainstay across various forms of media—ranging from books and movies to documentaries and podcasts. The enduring interest in the topic of serial killers is a testament to the profound impact these malevolent figures have had on the public's imagination.

At the core of this enduring fascination lies a morbid curiosity that beckons individuals to delve into the minds of those who commit unspeakable acts. The perennial questions surrounding the psychological underpinnings of their behavior act as a magnetic force, attracting both seasoned professionals and avid amateurs eager to navigate the intricate and twisted psyche of these killers. This collective quest for understanding becomes a journey into the darkest recesses of the human mind, seeking answers to the perennial question: what drives someone to commit such atrocities?

For true crime enthusiasts, the allure extends beyond the headlines, manifesting in an insatiable thirst for uncovering the intricate details of each case. From meticulously analyzing crime scenes to dissecting the modus operandi of the killers, these individuals embark on a relentless quest to unravel the enigma of the criminal mind. Each murder becomes a puzzle, waiting to be solved, and the more complex the case, the more irresistibly captivating it becomes—a captivating intellectual pursuit entwined with the quest for justice.

On the academic front, criminology students perceive the study of serial killers as an invaluable opportunity to gain profound insights into criminal behavior. The examination of patterns and motivations behind these heinous crimes is seen as a stepping stone toward contributing to the field of forensic psychology. As these students delve into the intricate web of motives, they aspire not only to understand the minds of serial killers but also to develop strategies for the prevention and intervention of such crimes.

Within the niche of serial killers, diverse subcategories further pique the interest of enthusiasts and students alike. Some are drawn to the chilling narratives of female serial killers—a minority yet equally haunting subgroup within the realm of serial murder. Others find themselves captivated by the unsolved cases, propelled by a sense of urgency for closure and justice. The specific modus operandi employed by certain killers, whether it be the methodical stranglers or the covert poisoners, becomes a focus for those intrigued by the intricacies of criminal behavior. Additionally, attention is directed toward the specific demographics targeted by these murderers, whether it be children, prostitutes, or other vulnerable groups—an exploration into the unsettling motivations behind these nefarious choices.

Moreover, the geographical aspect plays a pivotal role in amplifying the fascination with serial killers. The exploration of various regions or countries where these crimes have unfolded adds an extra layer of intrigue, transforming the location from a mere backdrop to an integral part of the narrative. From the foggy streets of Victorian London haunted by Jack the Ripper to the sun-drenched avenues of San Francisco terrorized by the Zodiac Killer, the setting becomes a character in its own right, influencing the unfolding drama.

The allure of serial killers is further amplified by those who have managed to elude capture—an unsolved mystery that adds to their infamy. The shadowy figures of unidentified killers cast a chilling veil over investigations, leaving both seasoned investigators and the public at large in suspense, wondering about the identity of these elusive culprits and when they might strike again.

In the pages of "Fatal Obsessions: A Journey into the Minds of Serial Killers," we invite readers to delve deep into this captivating world. The book offers a comprehensive examination that goes beyond the sensationalism, exploring the psychological profiles of these killers and unraveling the mysteries of unsolved cases. Whether you are a true crime enthusiast, a criminology student, or simply intrigued by the darker facets of the human psyche, this book stands as a must-read. Join us on this chilling journey as we attempt to unravel the enigma of serial killers and explore the profound hold they have on our collective consciousness.

Chapter 2

Female Serial Killers

Understanding the Motives and Characteristics of Female Serial Killers

In the labyrinth of serial killers, where the spotlight often gravitates toward male perpetrators, it becomes imperative to acknowledge the existence of female serial killers whose presence has left an indelible mark on history. This subchapter serves as a forensic exploration into the motives and characteristics of these often overlooked predators, casting a nuanced light on their distinctive psychological profiles.

While female serial killers may be fewer in number compared to their male counterparts, their motives and characteristics carve a unique path. In contrast to the power and control-driven motivations of male serial killers, their female counterparts often perpetrate heinous acts for different reasons. Although each case is inherently unique, discernible patterns emerge.

A significant motive among female serial killers is the pursuit of financial gain. These women frequently target vulnerable individuals, such as the elderly or infirm, employing methods such as poisoning or manipulation to secure insurance payouts or inheritances. The infamous "Angel of Death," Beverley Allitt, stands as a stark example, preying on children in her care to gain attention and sympathy while pursuing financial rewards.

Another motive manifesting among female serial killers is the psychological gratification derived from their crimes. Some become addicted to the rush and power felt when extinguishing another person's life. Their modus operandi may involve methods like strangulation or suffocation, providing a means to exert physical control and dominance over their victims. A chilling exemplar is Aileen Wuornos, who targeted and murdered multiple men, claiming self-defense but exhibiting a pattern of predatory behavior.

While male serial killers are often associated with targeting specific demographics, such as prostitutes or children, female serial killers exhibit similar preferences. Some specifically prey on vulnerable individuals, such as newborns or those in their care, as exemplified by the infamous "Baby Farmer," Amelia Dyer. Understanding these targeting patterns is imperative for developing profiles and implementing preventative measures.

It is crucial to note that not all female serial killers are apprehended and brought to justice. Their adeptness at blending into society and manipulating their surroundings often allows them to evade capture for extended periods. Unsolved cases, reminiscent of the "Doodler" or "Zodiac Killer," continue to intrigue both true crime enthusiasts and criminology students, fostering further exploration and analysis.

To comprehensively understand the motives and characteristics of female serial killers, a deep dive into their psychological profiles is essential. This subchapter endeavors to illuminate the complex nature of these individuals, enabling true crime enthusiasts and criminology students to glean a profound understanding of the disconcerting world inhabited by female serial killers. By unraveling their motives and characteristics, strides can be taken toward preventing future acts of violence and safeguarding potential victims.

Infamous Cases of Female Serial Killers

Introduction:

In the ominous realm of serial killers, the narratives of female perpetrators often linger in the shadows cast by their male counterparts. However, the chilling and disturbing stories of these women deserve equal attention. This subchapter embarks on an exploration of the captivating and horrifying cases of female serial killers, unveiling their motivations, methods, and psychological profiles. From poisoners to stranglers, these women have woven a tapestry of death and terror.

1. The Black Widow: Belle Gunness

Belle Gunness, known as the "Black Widow," cast a dark shadow over the Midwest during the early 20th century. This Norwegian immigrant lured unsuspecting men through lonely hearts ads, orchestrating their murders for financial gain. Her gruesome crimes remained concealed until a fire engulfed her farmhouse, laying bare a graveyard of dismembered bodies.

2. The Angel of Death: Beverley Allitt

Beverley Allitt, a British nurse, assumed the guise of an angel as she preyed upon vulnerable patients under her care. Administering lethal doses of insulin and other medications, she caused the deaths of several children and left numerous others severely disabled. Allitt's twisted desire for attention and power ultimately led to her capture and conviction.

3. The Monster of the Andes: Luisa Toledo

Luisa Toledo, also known as the "Monster of the Andes," sent shockwaves across the world with her unimaginable crimes. Operating in South America, she targeted young girls, subjecting them to sexual assault and murder with sadistic pleasure. Toledo's ability to evade capture for years highlighted the formidable challenges faced by law enforcement agencies in tracking down female serial killers.

4. The Giggling Granny: Nannie Doss

Nannie Doss, dubbed the "Giggling Granny," presented herself as an ordinary housewife. However, beneath her cheerful facade lurked a deadly secret. Doss poisoned multiple family members, including husbands, children, and even her own mother. Her motive? A twisted desire for attention and the pursuit of an elusive perfect husband.

Conclusion:

These infamous cases of female serial killers unveil the complex and often overlooked world of women who commit heinous crimes. Their motivations, methods, and psychological profiles are as diverse as those of their male counterparts. True crime enthusiasts and criminology students will find these stories simultaneously captivating and disturbing, providing a glimpse into the dark facets of human nature. Whether intrigued by the psychology of serial killers or drawn to unsolved cases, this subchapter invites readers to confront the terrifying reality that evil

Chapter 3

Unsolved Serial Killings

The Mystery Behind Unsolved Serial Killings

In the ominous depths of true crime, few subjects evoke as much intrigue among enthusiasts and criminology students as unsolved serial killings. These haunting cases, permanently etched in the annals of criminal history, perpetually bewilder investigators and cast a somber shadow over the families of victims. What compels these elusive predators to operate covertly for extended periods, leaving behind a trail of terror? In "Fatal Obsessions: A Journey into the Minds of Serial Killers," we embark on a profound exploration of the enigmatic world of unsolved serial killings, illuminating the darkest recesses of the human psyche.

The term "serial killers" itself elicits shivers, captivating our collective imagination. The concept of these perpetrators targeting specific demographics or employing distinctive modus operandi, such as strangulation or poisoning, adds an extra layer of complexity to their sinister deeds. Our book meticulously unravels the chilling narratives of serial killers who preyed on children, prostitutes, or operated within specific regions or countries. By delving into these cases, our objective is to unveil the convoluted reasoning behind their choice of victims and methods, providing readers with a profound insight into the twisted minds of these predators.

While some serial killers have been apprehended and subjected to psychological profiling, others have eluded capture, leaving behind a web of unanswered questions. Our subchapter on unsolved serial killings guides readers through some of history's most confounding cases. From the notorious Zodiac Killer to the elusive Jack the Ripper, we scrutinize the myriad theories and suspects that have surfaced over the years, empowering readers to formulate their own conclusions. The tantalizing prospect of these murderers walking among us, their identities yet concealed, ensures that true crime enthusiasts and criminology students are left pondering the mysteries that endure.

Famous Unsolved Serial Killings and the Impact on Society

In the cryptic underbelly of the criminal world, a breed of predators—serial killers—haunts the collective imagination of society. While many of these twisted individuals have faced justice, there exist some whose crimes remain unsolved, casting a haunting veil of unanswered questions and unfulfilled justice. This subchapter immerses itself in the enigmatic realm of famous unsolved serial killings, exploring the profound impact they have had on society.

For true crime enthusiasts and criminology students, the allure of unsolved serial killings is irresistible. These cases offer a unique lens into the minds of these disturbed individuals, challenging our understanding of criminal psychology and investigative techniques. By examining these mysteries, we gain a deeper appreciation for the complexities involved in solving such heinous crimes.

Jack the Ripper:

One case that continues to captivate the public's attention is the infamous Jack the Ripper murders. This unidentified serial killer terrorized the streets of London's Whitechapel district in the late 1800s, targeting vulnerable women and leaving a trail of mutilated bodies in his wake. Despite an extensive investigation and numerous theories, Jack the Ripper's true identity has never been conclusively determined. The enduring fascination with this case stems from its historical significance, marking the emergence of modern forensic techniques and the birth of the public's morbid fascination with serial killers.

The Zodiac Killer:

Another intriguing unsolved case is the Zodiac Killer, who plagued the San Francisco Bay Area in the late 1960s and early 1970s. With cryptic letters and taunting messages to the media, the Zodiac Killer struck fear into the hearts of the public. Despite an intense investigation and countless suspects, the killer's identity remains unknown. This case not only underscores the limitations of forensic technology at the time but also showcases the power of a charismatic and elusive killer who can manipulate both the media and the public's imagination.

Impact on Society:

The impact of unsolved serial killings extends beyond mere fascination. These cases often expose flaws in law enforcement procedures, leading to reforms in investigative techniques and the development of new forensic technologies. They also shed light on societal issues, such as the vulnerability of certain demographics, such as children or sex workers, and the challenges faced by investigators in catching elusive killers who operate within specific regions or countries.

By exploring the psychological profiles of these unsolved serial killers, we gain a deeper understanding of the complex motivations that drive such heinous acts. Whether it is the stranglers, poisoners, or those targeting specific demographics, these cases offer valuable insights into the darkest corners of the human mind.

Conclusion:

"Fatal Obsessions: A Journey into the Minds of Serial Killers" emerges as an essential read for true crime enthusiasts, criminology students, and anyone fascinated by the twisted world of serial killers. By delving into famous unsolved cases and their impact on society, this subchapter offers a chilling yet captivating exploration of the unresolved mysteries that continue to haunt us to this day.

Expanded Section: The Role of Technology in Solving Unsolved Cases

In the realm of true crime, unsolved cases exert an undeniable allure over the minds of both true crime enthusiasts and criminology students. These cases, adorned with elusive culprits and lingering questions, have long fascinated the public. However, the advent of technology has opened new doors in the relentless pursuit of justice. This subchapter delves into the indispensable role that technology plays in solving unsolved cases, with a particular focus on serial killers and their chilling crimes.

One of the most monumental advancements in recent years is the advent of DNA analysis. By scrutinizing the genetic material left at crime scenes, investigators can now identify perpetrators with unprecedented accuracy. This breakthrough has empowered law enforcement agencies to link previously unrelated crimes, unveiling patterns and connections that were once hidden. For true crime enthusiasts and criminology students, this translates to a deeper understanding of the motivations and modus operandi of serial killers.

Even female serial killers, often overlooked in traditional crime narratives, have reaped the benefits of technological advancements. Through the use of DNA evidence, investigators have unmasked these deadly women who operated in the shadows, shedding light on their psychological profiles and the unique factors that drove them to kill. This newfound knowledge is invaluable in understanding the complexities of criminal behavior.

Furthermore, technology has played a pivotal role

in solving cold cases where killers seemed to have eluded capture for decades. In recent years, advancements in forensic science and digital databases have enabled investigators to re-examine evidence and discover new leads. Serial killers who once believed they had escaped justice for their heinous crimes are now being apprehended. For enthusiasts of unsolved serial killings, this is an exhilarating era as fresh information and theories come to light.

Additionally, technology has become a potent tool in profiling serial killers based on their specific modus operandi or target demographics. By analyzing crime scene data and employing sophisticated algorithms, investigators can anticipate the killer's next move, potentially preventing future tragedies. This cutting-edge approach to crime-solving has revolutionized the field of criminology, offering valuable insights to both students and true crime enthusiasts.

In conclusion, the role of technology in solving unsolved cases cannot be overstated. From DNA analysis to digital databases and profiling techniques, technology has transformed the way we approach criminal investigations, especially in the realm of serial killers. For true crime enthusiasts and criminology students, these advancements provide a deeper understanding of the psychological profiles, motivations, and patterns of these elusive killers. As technology continues to evolve, the breakthroughs and revelations it will bring to the world of true crime are boundless.

Chapter 4

Serial Killers with Specific Modus Operandi

A Closer Look at Serial Killers Who Strangle Their Victims

Introduction:

In the shadowy realms of serial killers, a distinct category of murderers with a chilling modus operandi emerges—the stranglers. These individuals, both male and female, have etched an indelible mark on the annals of criminal history, fascinating and horrifying true crime enthusiasts, criminology students, and anyone intrigued by the disturbing minds of serial killers. In this subchapter of "Fatal Obsessions: A Journey into the Minds of Serial Killers," we embark on a profound exploration of the terrifying world of stranglers, unraveling their methods, motives, and psychological profiles.

Exploring Infamous Cases:

Stranglers, ranging from notorious figures like Ted Bundy and Aileen Wuornos to lesser-known yet equally twisted killers like Gerard Schaefer and Martha Beck, leave a haunting imprint on criminal history. By delving into their cases, we aim to unveil the psychological intricacies driving stranglers to commit heinous acts repeatedly. Meticulous research and analysis shed light not only on the criminal minds of these stranglers but also on the factors contributing to their specific choice of modus operandi.

Understanding Psychological Significance:

We delve into the unique characteristics of strangulation as a murder method and its psychological significance for the perpetrators. The patterns and behaviors exhibited by stranglers, including their choice of victims, locations, and the aftermath of their crimes, are meticulously examined. By understanding the intricacies of their actions, we offer readers a comprehensive insight into the twisted rationale behind the act of strangulation.

Unsolved Cases:

For enthusiasts fascinated by unsolved serial killings, we delve into the cases of stranglers who managed to evade capture, leaving a trail of fear and unanswered questions. Examination of these unsolved mysteries aims to spark discussions and theories among true crime enthusiasts and criminology students, encouraging active engagement in the pursuit of justice for the victims and their families.

Conclusion:

Whether intrigued by the psychology behind serial killers, fascinated by the unsolved mysteries they leave in their wake, or simply seeking a deeper understanding of these dark figures, this subchapter on stranglers promises to captivate and disturb. Join us on this chilling journey into the minds of those who choose to prey on their victims using the terrifying method of strangulation.

The Deadly World of Serial Killers Who Use Poison

Introduction:

In the obscure underbelly of the world of serial killers, a nefarious group of individuals lurks in the shadows, wielding a silent and insidious weapon—poison. These cunning murderers possess a unique set of skills and a disturbing fascination with the art of killing with toxic substances. In this subchapter, we plunge into the chilling world of poisoners, exploring their methods, motives, and the psychology behind their deadly obsession.

Captivating the True Crime World:

Poisoners have long captivated the true crime world with their ability to blend into society, unsuspected, while leaving a trail of death and destruction. Unlike other serial killers who rely on brute force or manipulation, poisoners excel in the art of subtlety. Carefully selecting their victims, often targeting the vulnerable or those who trust them implicitly, they wield a range of poisons, from arsenic and cyanide to more unconventional substances like belladonna or thallium.

Evading Capture:

One of the most intriguing aspects of poisoners is their ability to evade capture for extended periods. Unlike other killers who leave behind a physical trace, poisoners are known for their meticulous planning and methodical approach. This subchapter explores some of the most notorious poisoners who were never caught, leaving a trail of unsolved serial killings that continue to baffle criminologists and law enforcement agencies.

Psychological Profiles:

Furthermore, we delve into the unique psychological profiles of these poisoners. What drives these individuals to turn to such a deadly method of killing? What are the underlying motivations and personality traits that distinguish them from other types of serial killers? Through in-depth analysis and case studies, we aim to shed light on the twisted minds behind these lethal acts.

Comprehensive Exploration:

For true crime enthusiasts and criminology students, this subchapter provides a comprehensive exploration of poisoners and their deadly world. We unravel the chilling stories of female serial killers who utilized poison as their weapon of choice, as well as those who targeted specific demographics, such as children or prostitutes. Additionally, we examine poisoners from different regions and countries, highlighting the unique cultural influences on their crimes.

Conclusion:

"Poisoners: The Deadly World of Serial Killers Who Use Poison" takes readers on a dark journey into the minds of these enigmatic killers. With meticulous research, gripping case studies, and psychological analysis, this subchapter is an essential read for those fascinated by the intricate workings of serial killers and their insidious methods.

Serial Killers and Their Signature Methods of Killing

Introduction:

One of the most intriguing aspects of the world of serial killers lies in the unique and chilling methods they employ to carry out their heinous acts. In this subchapter, we delve into the twisted minds of these killers and explore their signature methods of killing. From stranglers to poisoners, this section provides a comprehensive look at the various techniques adopted by these individuals to perpetrate their crimes.

Understanding Stranglers:

Stranglers, notorious for their ability to overpower their victims, leave behind a distinctive mark on their victims' bodies. We examine the psychology behind this method, exploring the power dynamics and control issues that drive these killers to choose such a hands-on approach. Additionally, we delve into the techniques employed by these stranglers, shedding light on the intricacies of their craft.

Insidious World of Poisoners:

Poisoners, on the other hand, operate in a more clandestine and covert manner. Their weapon of choice is often an undetectable substance that silently takes the lives of their unsuspecting victims. We explore the dark world of poisoners, unraveling their motivations and delving into the complex psychology that drives them to commit these secretive acts. From toxicology to forensic analysis, we provide an in-depth understanding of the science and techniques behind poisonings.

Targeting Specific Demographics:

Furthermore, we delve into the chilling realm of serial killers who target specific demographics. Whether it be children or prostitutes, these killers select their victims based on specific characteristics. We examine the factors that contribute to these choices and explore the motives that drive these killers to single out particular groups.

Unsolved Cases:

In addition to discussing the well-known serial killers who have been caught, we also shed light on those who have managed to evade capture. By examining unsolved serial killings, we offer insights into the challenges faced by law enforcement agencies in bringing these individuals to justice. We explore the reasons behind their elusiveness and discuss the potential psychological profiles that could aid in their identification.

Conclusion:

By delving into the minds of serial killers and dissecting their signature methods of killing, "Fatal Obsessions: A Journey into the Minds of Serial Killers" provides a comprehensive and captivating exploration for true crime enthusiasts and criminology students alike. This subchapter caters to the interests of those intrigued by the psychology of serial killers, as well as those fascinated by the unsolved mysteries that continue to haunt the world of criminal investigation.

Chapter 5

Serial Killers Targeting Specific Demographics

Children as Victims: Serial Killers Who Prey on the Innocent

In the harrowing world of serial killers, a particularly distressing phenomenon emerges—individuals who stoop to unimaginable depths by targeting the most vulnerable members of society: children. This sub-chapter delves into the chilling reality of serial killers who specifically prey on the innocent, exploring their motives, methods, and the psychological profiles that drive them to commit these heinous acts.

Understanding the Motives:

Serial killers who target children often harbor unique motives that set them apart from other murderers. Some are driven by a sadistic desire for power and control over those who are defenseless. Others may have unresolved childhood trauma or perverted fantasies involving children. Additionally, some offenders may believe that killing children will allow them to evade suspicion or capture by the authorities.

Methods and Modus Operandi:

The methods employed by serial killers who victimize children can vary widely, reflecting the individual preferences of the offender. Some may employ physical violence, while others rely on manipulation and coercion. Certain killers may choose specific modus operandi, such as strangulation or poisoning, to satisfy their sadistic desires or maintain a sense of control over their victims.

Psychological Profiles:

Understanding the psychological profiles of serial killers who target children provides insight into their distorted minds. These individuals may exhibit traits such as narcissism, antisocial personality disorder, or pedophilic tendencies. Exploring the psychological underpinnings of these offenders can help criminology students and true crime enthusiasts gain a deeper understanding of the motivations behind their crimes.

Unsolved Serial Killings and the Impact on Communities:

Unfortunately, not all serial killers who prey on children are apprehended, leaving communities in a state of fear and uncertainty. This section delves into unsolved cases, examining the challenges faced by law enforcement in capturing these elusive predators and the lasting impact on the affected communities.

"Children as Victims: Serial Killers Who Prey on the Innocent" sheds light on a particularly distressing aspect of serial killing. By exploring the motives, methods, and psychological profiles of these offenders, true crime enthusiasts and criminology students can gain a deeper understanding of the dark forces that drive individuals to commit such horrifying acts. Furthermore, examining unsolved cases and their impact on communities highlights the urgent need for continued research and investigation to bring justice to the victims and their families.

Prostitutes: Serial Killers and the Dark World of Sex Workers

In the underbelly of society, where darkness and

despair converge, a chilling reality persists: the world of prostitutes and the serial killers who prey upon them. This subchapter delves into the macabre and disturbing connection between these two entities, shedding light on the oft-ignored victims and the twisted minds that perpetrate these heinous crimes.

Vulnerability of Prostitutes:

Prostitutes have long been a vulnerable and marginalized group, often forced into the trade by circumstances beyond their control. Their dangerous line of work exposes them to a myriad of risks, including robbery, assault, and, tragically, murder. Serial killers, with their insatiable bloodlust and warped desires, view these sex workers as easy prey, exploiting their precarious situations for their own sadistic pleasure.

Female Serial Killers Turned Perpetrators:

The stories of female serial killers who were once sex workers themselves are particularly haunting. Driven by a toxic cocktail of trauma, rage, and a thirst for revenge, they transform from victims to perpetrators, exacting their twisted justice on unsuspecting clients. These women navigate the dark recesses of the sex industry, using their intimate knowledge to lure and dispatch their victims, leaving a trail of bodies in their wake.

Unsolved Cases and Systemic Challenges:

Unsolved serial killings involving prostitutes form a haunting tapestry of unspeakable crimes. These cases, shrouded in mystery, often reveal the deep-seated biases and negligence of law enforcement agencies and society at large. The victims, dismissed as disposable, face a justice system that fails them time and time again. The subchapter explores these cases, shedding light on the victims' lives and the desperate search for justice that continues to this day.

Modus Operandi of Serial Killers:

This subchapter also examines the unique modus operandi of serial killers who target sex workers. From stranglers to poisoners, these sadistic individuals employ specific methods to exert control and dominance over their victims. By analyzing these patterns, criminology students and true crime enthusiasts can gain a deeper understanding of the psychology behind these gruesome acts.

Geographical and Demographic Aspects:

Furthermore, this subchapter delves into the geographical and demographic aspects of serial killers who target prostitutes. From the Green River Killer's reign of terror in the United States to the haunting cases of the Yorkshire Ripper in the United Kingdom, these serial killers leave a lasting impact on their respective regions. By exploring these cases, readers can gain insight into the unique challenges faced by law enforcement agencies when dealing with these elusive killers.

In conclusion, "Prostitutes: Serial Killers and the Dark World of Sex Workers" exposes the terrifying reality faced by those who inhabit the shadowy realms of the sex industry. By examining the cases of both the killers and their victims, this subchapter aims to shed light on the deep psychological and societal factors that contribute to these horrifying crimes. For true crime enthusiasts, criminology students, and those fascinated by the intricate web of serial killers, this exploration into the dark world of sex workers is sure to captivate and disturb.

Serial Killers and Their Obsession with Targeting Specific Groups

One of the most intriguing aspects of serial killers and their crimes is their obsession with targeting specific groups. Whether it be children, prostitutes, or individuals belonging to a particular region or country, these killers develop a fixation on a certain demographic that drives their murderous actions. In this chapter, we will delve into the twisted minds of these murderers and explore the reasons behind their obsession.

Psychological Insights:

Serial killers often choose their victims based on specific characteristics that they find appealing or vulnerable. For example, some killers are drawn to children due to their innocence and the power they feel when robbing them of their lives. Others target prostitutes, viewing them as disposable individuals who won't be missed. By focusing on specific groups, these killers believe they can evade detection for longer periods.

Female Serial Killers:

Female serial killers, although less common than their male counterparts, also develop a fascination with particular demographics. Some female killers become known as "angels of death" by targeting vulnerable patients in hospitals or nursing homes. These sinister individuals exploit their positions of trust to carry out their heinous acts. Understanding their motives can provide valuable insights into their psychological profiles.

Unsolved Cases and Challenges:

Unsolved serial killings present an even more perplexing puzzle. These cases leave investigators and true crime enthusiasts searching for answers, wondering why certain demographics were targeted and how the killer managed to evade capture. Examining these unsolved cases can shed light on the challenges faced by law enforcement agencies and the unique characteristics of these unidentified killers.

Signature Modus Operandi:

Additionally, some serial killers adopt specific modus operandi, such as strangling or poisoning their victims. These murderers become fixated on a particular method, often driven by a need for control or a desire to inflict specific types of suffering. Exploring these patterns can help criminology students understand the mindsets of these killers and their motivations.

Geographical and Cultural Influences:

Serial killers operating in specific regions or countries also present an interesting study. Cultural, social, and environmental factors can influence the choice of victims and the manner in which these killers carry out their crimes. By examining these cases, we can gain a deeper understanding of the complex relationship between a killer and their surroundings.

The Chilling World of Unsolved Cases:

Lastly, we will explore the chilling world of serial killers who were never caught. These elusive murderers continue to haunt the public's imagination, leaving behind a trail of unsolved crimes. Analyzing their psychological profiles and examining their crimes can offer valuable insights into the challenges faced by law enforcement and the importance of early detection and prevention.

Conclusion:

In this chapter, we will delve into the disturbing minds of serial killers who develop obsessions with targeting specific groups. By exploring these cases and their psychological profiles, we hope to shed light on the motives behind their actions and provide a deeper understanding of this dark and disturbing aspect of criminal behavior.

Chapter 6

Serial Killers Operating in Specific Regions or Countries

The United States: Notorious Serial Killers and Their Hunting Grounds

The United States has been haunted by the chilling presence of notorious serial killers, individuals who have left a trail of terror and devastation across the nation. This subchapter delves into the dark and twisted minds of these killers, exploring their hunting grounds and the gruesome crimes they committed. From stranglers to poisoners, from those targeting specific demographics to those operating in specific regions, we will uncover the macabre tales that have both fascinated and horrified true crime enthusiasts, criminology students, and those intrigued by the psychological profiles of these murderers.

Ted Bundy:

One infamous serial killer that haunts the annals of American history is Ted Bundy. Known for his charm and good looks, Bundy preyed upon young women, often luring them with his charismatic persona. His hunting grounds spanned across several states, including Washington, Oregon, Utah, and Florida. With his carefully calculated modus operandi, he would abduct his victims, subjecting them to unspeakable horrors before ultimately taking their lives. Despite his capture and subsequent execution, the true extent of Bundy's crimes remains unknown, leaving many unsolved cases in his wake.

Aileen Wuornos:

Another chilling example is Aileen Wuornos, a female serial killer who targeted men along the highways of Florida. Wuornos, a prostitute herself, became infamous for her methodical killings, claiming that she acted in self-defense against abusive clients. Her psychological profile provides a unique insight into the mind of a female serial killer, raising questions about the intersection of gender, trauma, and violence.

Richard Ramirez - The "Night Stalker":

Moving to a different type of serial killer, we encounter the likes of Richard Ramirez, known as the "Night Stalker." Ramirez terrorized the residents of Los Angeles, committing a series of home invasions and brutal murders. With a preference for targeting elderly individuals, Ramirez struck fear into the hearts of Californians, leaving behind a wake of bloodshed and carnage.

Exploration and Psychological Profiles:

As we explore these notorious cases and the regions in which they unfolded, we uncover the dark underbelly of American society. We examine the psychological profiles of these killers, attempting to understand the twisted motivations that drove them to commit these heinous acts. For true crime enthusiasts, criminology students, and those captivated by the enigma of serial killers, this subchapter offers a chilling glimpse into the minds of these monsters and the haunting hunting grounds they called home.

Europe: Infamous Serial Killers and Their Terrifying Legacies

Europe has witnessed its fair share of notorious serial killers, leaving behind a trail of horror and terror.

In this chapter, we delve into the dark and twisted minds of Europe's most infamous serial killers, exploring their unique modus operandi, their victims, and the chilling legacies they left behind.

The Stranglers: Unleashing Fear and Death:

1. Europe has witnessed its fair share of serial killers who derive pleasure from strangulation. From Jack the Ripper in Victorian London to Peter Sutcliffe, the Yorkshire Ripper, these killers have targeted vulnerable women, leaving communities paralyzed with fear. We explore their psychological profiles, their hunting grounds, and the long-lasting impact on society.

Poisoners: Silent Killers Among Us:

2. Some of Europe's most chilling killers have employed poison as their weapon of choice, often targeting unsuspecting victims. We delve into the twisted minds of infamous poisoners like Graham Young and Catherine Birnie, examining their motivations, methods, and the psychological factors that contributed to their deadly obsessions.

Children and Prostitutes: Preying on the Vulnerable:

3. Serial killers often focus their attention on specific demographics, exploiting their vulnerabilities.

We delve into the haunting cases of Ian Brady and Myra Hindley, who targeted children, and the infamous "Monster of Florence," who preyed on prostitutes. Through psychological analysis, we attempt to understand the motives behind these heinous crimes and the impact on their victims' communities.

Unsolved Serial Killings: The Haunting Mysteries:

4. Europe is no stranger to unsolved serial killings, leaving communities in a perpetual state of fear and uncertainty. From the "Zodiac Killer" in 1960s and 70s San Francisco to the "Phantom of Heilbronn" in Germany, we explore these baffling cases, examining the evidence, the suspects, and the enduring legacies they have left behind.

Serial Killers Who Were Never Caught: Escaping Justice:

5. While some serial killers are eventually brought to justice, others manage to evade capture, leaving law enforcement agencies and communities frustrated and fearful. We delve into the chilling cases of infamous killers like the "Mad Butcher of Kingsbury Run" and the "Axeman of New Orleans," exploring the reasons behind their elusiveness and the psychological profiles of these cunning predators.

Europe's history is stained with the bloodshed caused by notorious serial killers. Their terrifying legacies continue to captivate the minds of true crime enthusiasts and criminology students alike. By examining their modus operandi, psychological profiles, and the impact they had on their victims and society, we hope to shed light on the darkness that resides within these individuals and prevent such horrors from repeating in the future.

Serial Killers and their Impact on Different Countries

Serial killers have left an indelible mark on societies across the globe, their crimes creating shockwaves that reverberate through the history of various countries. This subchapter delves into the haunting tales of serial killers from different regions, exploring their modus operandi, the demographics they targeted, and the psychological profiles that defined their monstrous actions. From the United States to Europe, from Asia to South America, each region has its own unique stories to tell.

United States:

In the United States, infamous names like Ted Bundy, Jeffrey Dahmer, and John Wayne Gacy have become synonymous with the horrors of serial killing. These men, driven by their own twisted desires, targeted different demographics, from young boys to vulnerable women, leaving communities in a state of perpetual fear. Their psychological profiles offer a chilling glimpse into the minds of these monsters, shedding light on the complex factors that led to their deadly obsessions.

Europe:

Moving across the Atlantic, Europe has its own share of notorious serial killers. Jack the Ripper, haunting the streets of Victorian London, remains one of the most enigmatic and infamous figures in criminal history. His brutal murders of prostitutes and his ability to evade capture have made him a subject of fascination for true crime enthusiasts and criminology students alike. Similarly, the "Monster of Florence" terrorized Italy for years, targeting couples and leaving a trail of bodies in his wake. These cases highlight the cultural and historical context within which these killers operated, reshaping the perception of safety in these regions.

Asia:

Venturing further to Asia, countries like Japan and South Korea have faced their own serial killers. The "Tsuyama massacre" in Japan and the "Hwaseong serial murders" in South Korea shocked these nations, as the killers targeted specific demographics and employed unique methods of murder. These cases offer valuable insights into the cultural and societal factors that contribute to the development of serial killers in these regions.

Australia and South America:

From Australia's backpacker murders to South America's "Death Squad" killings, each region has its own dark tales to share. The impact of these serial killers on their countries is multifaceted, leaving lasting scars on the collective conscience. Understanding their modus operandi, the demographics they targeted, and the psychological profiles that drove them is crucial in unraveling the complexities of these crimes.

For true crime enthusiasts and criminology students, this subchapter provides a comprehensive exploration of serial killers operating in different regions. By examining the specific contexts within which these killers thrived, readers gain a deeper understanding of the psychological, social, and cultural factors that contribute to the creation of these monsters. Through this exploration, we hope to shed light on these dark corners of human psychology and ultimately, contribute to the prevention and detection of future serial killers.

Chapter 7

Serial Killers Who Were Never Caught

The Elusive Killers: Famous Cases of Serial Killers Who Evaded Capture

In the dark and twisted realm of true crime, there exists a chilling subset of killers who have managed to elude justice, slipping through the cracks of law enforcement's grasp. These enigmatic figures have baffled investigators, leaving behind a trail of unsolved mysteries and shattered lives. In this subchapter, we delve into the haunting tales of serial killers who evaded capture, examining their chilling crimes and the psychological profiles that shaped their deadly obsessions.

Unsolved Serial Killings:

The annals of true crime are filled with unsolved serial killings that continue to haunt investigators and communities alike. From the infamous Jack the Ripper, who terrorized the streets of Victorian London with a macabre savagery, to the Zodiac Killer, who taunted authorities with cryptic messages, these cases have captivated the public's imagination for decades. We explore the methods, motives, and potential identities of these elusive killers, dissecting the evidence and theories surrounding their crimes.

Serial Killers Targeting Specific Demographics:

Some serial killers develop a chilling preference for specific demographics, unleashing their wrath upon the most vulnerable members of society. From child murderers like Westley Allan Dodd to the Grim Sleeper, who preyed upon prostitutes in Los Angeles, these predators exploit societal vulnerabilities to carry out their heinous acts. We examine the underlying motivations and modus operandi of such killers, shedding light on the terrifying intersections of power, control, and deviance.

Serial Killers Operating in Specific Regions or Countries:

Serial killers are not confined to any particular

borders, and their reigns of terror often transcend geographical boundaries. From the Green River Killer, who plagued the Pacific Northwest, to the Monster of Florence, who stalked the Italian countryside, we explore the chilling tales of these killers and the unique challenges they posed to law enforcement agencies. By delving into the geography and cultural contexts of these cases, we gain a deeper understanding of the complexities involved in capturing these elusive murderers.

The Psychology of Serial Killers:

What drives an individual to become a serial killer? This question has fascinated criminology students and true crime enthusiasts for decades. In this sub-chapter, we delve into the psychological profiles of some of history's most notorious killers, from the charming and manipulative Ted Bundy to the meticulous and sadistic Dennis Rader, also known as the BTK Killer. By examining their childhoods, personal histories, and patterns of behavior, we seek to understand the twisted minds behind their fatal obsessions.

The world of serial killers is a dark and disturbing realm, populated by individuals who have managed to evade justice. Their crimes continue to captivate and terrify us, leaving behind a legacy of unanswered questions and shattered lives. In Fatal Obsessions: A Journey into the Minds of Serial Killers, we explore the chilling tales of these elusive killers, shedding light on their methods, motives, and the psychological factors that shaped their murderous obsessions. Whether you are a true crime enthusiast, a criminology student, or simply intrigued by the enigma of the human mind, this subchapter will provide you with an unsettling glimpse into the twisted world of serial killers who evaded capture.

The Challenges in Investigating and Apprehending Serial Killers

Introduction:

For true crime enthusiasts and criminology students, the world of serial killers is a fascinating yet chilling subject. Delving into the minds of these murderers brings forth a multitude of questions and challenges that law enforcement faces when attempting to investigate and apprehend them. In this subchapter, we will explore the various obstacles that hinder the process of catching these elusive criminals.

Remaining Undetected:

One of the foremost challenges in apprehending serial killers is their ability to remain undetected for extended periods. The cunning nature of these individuals often allows them to blend into society seamlessly, making it difficult for law enforcement to identify them as potential suspects. This is particularly true for female serial killers, who are often underestimated due to societal stereotypes. Understanding the psychological profiles of these killers and recognizing the signs of their behavior patterns can aid investigators in narrowing down their list of suspects.

Unsolved Serial Killings:

Another significant challenge arises when dealing with unsolved serial killings. These cases continue to haunt law enforcement agencies and communities, leaving victims' families without closure. The lack of evidence, witnesses, or even leads makes the investigation arduous and frustrating. However, advancements in forensic science and DNA profiling techniques offer hope for resolving previously unsolved cases, providing a glimmer of justice for the victims and their loved ones.

Specific Modus Operandi:

Serial killers with specific modus operandi, such as stranglers or poisoners, pose unique challenges to investigators. Their chosen method of killing may not leave behind visible evidence, making it harder to connect the dots and establish a pattern. Additionally, their specific choice of victims, such as children or prostitutes, may make the investigation more complex due to the marginalized nature of these demographics. Overcoming biases and ensuring equal attention and resources are dedicated to these cases are critical steps towards apprehending these killers.

Operating in Specific Regions or Countries:

Operating in specific regions or countries, serial killers may exploit jurisdictional boundaries, making coordination between law enforcement agencies difficult. Lack of cooperation and information sharing can impede progress and hinder the investigation. Establishing effective communication channels and collaboration between agencies is essential in bringing these criminals to justice.

Serial Killers Who Were Never Caught:

Finally, the most perplexing challenge of all is the serial killer who was never caught. These elusive predators often leave law enforcement scratching their heads, as they seem to effortlessly evade capture. Uncovering their motives, understanding their modus operandi, and developing new investigative techniques are vital in the ongoing quest to apprehend these unidentified killers.

In conclusion, investigating and apprehending serial killers is an intricate and demanding task. As true crime enthusiasts and criminology students, understanding the challenges faced by law enforcement in these cases is crucial. By examining the complexities involved in identifying, investigating, and ultimately capturing these killers, we can gain valuable insights into the dark recesses of their minds and work towards preventing future tragedies.

The Unsolved Mysteries and Consequences of Unsolved Cases

In the dark and twisted realm of serial killers, there exists a haunting subset of cases that continue to baffle investigators and leave the public in a state of perpetual unease. These are the unsolved mysteries, the enigmatic crimes that have eluded capture and left a trail of unanswered questions in their wake. As we delve into the depths of these unsolved cases, we are confronted with the chilling reality that some killers may forever remain hidden amongst us.

The Allure of Unsolved Serial Killings:

For true crime enthusiasts and criminology students alike, the allure of unsolved serial killings is undeniable. These cases offer a unique glimpse into the minds of these elusive predators, providing a tantalizing challenge for those who seek to understand the motivations and methods behind their heinous acts. From female serial killers to those with specific modus operandi, such as stranglers or poisoners, the unsolved mysteries encompass a diverse range of criminal profiles.

Specific Demographics and Consequences:

One of the most disturbing aspects of these unsolved cases is the specific demographics that some serial killers target. Whether it be children or prostitutes, these vulnerable groups become the unfortunate prey of these sadistic individuals. The consequences of these unsolved crimes extend far beyond the initial victims, as fear and paranoia seep into the very fabric of society. Communities are left grappling with the knowledge that a predator roams among them, their sense of security forever shattered.

Operating Within Specific Regions or Countries:

Operating within specific regions or countries, some serial killers have managed to evade capture for decades, leaving a trail of fear and destruction in their wake. These unsolved cases serve as a grim reminder that justice is not always swift, and that even the most meticulous investigations can falter in the face of an elusive killer. The psychological profiles of these unidentified murderers offer a chilling insight into the depths of human depravity, as we attempt to understand what drives them to commit such heinous acts.

Concluding Thoughts:

As we navigate the treacherous territory of unsolved serial killings, it becomes apparent that these cases transcend mere fascination; they serve as a stark reminder of the fragility of human life. The unsolved mysteries and their consequences are a chilling testament to the darkness that resides within our society, and an urgent call to action to ensure that these predators are brought to justice. Only by shining a light into the shadows can we hope to unravel the secrets of these unsolved cases and bring solace to the victims and their families.

Chapter 8

Serial Killers and Their Psychological Profiles

The Minds of Serial Killers: Understanding the Psychological Motivations

Serial killers have long captivated the public's imagination, leaving us both fascinated and repulsed by their heinous crimes. In "Fatal Obsessions: A Journey into the Minds of Serial Killers," we delve deep into the twisted psyche of these individuals, exploring their psychological motivations and shedding light on the dark recesses of their minds.

Gender Differences:

For true crime enthusiasts and criminology students alike, understanding the psychological underpinnings of serial killers is essential to comprehending the complex nature of their crimes. By unraveling the intricate web of their thoughts, emotions, and desires, we gain valuable insights into the factors that drive these individuals to commit such horrific acts.

One aspect that particularly intrigues researchers is the stark contrast between male and female serial killers. While males tend to display more violent and impulsive behavior, females often employ cunning manipulation and emotional manipulation to achieve their deadly goals. Exploring the gender differences in serial killing can provide invaluable knowledge for those studying criminology or seeking to understand the dynamics of these crimes.

Exploration of Unsolved Serial Killings:

Furthermore, our book shines a light on unsolved serial killings, those haunting cases that continue to baffle investigators and leave communities in fear. By examining these cold cases, we aim to shed new light on the possible motives and psychological profiles of the perpetrators, offering fresh perspectives and potential breakthroughs that could finally bring justice to the victims and closure to their families.

Specific Modus Operandi and Target Demographics:

Our exploration of serial killers with specific modus operandi, such as stranglers or poisoners, delves into the unique psychological makeup of these individuals. By understanding their chosen method of killing, we gain insight into their motives, fantasies, and underlying psychological needs, which can prove invaluable in the investigation and prevention of future crimes.

Additionally, we examine serial killers who target specific demographics, such as children or prostitutes. By understanding the factors that drive these individuals to prey on vulnerable populations, we can develop strategies to protect potential victims and apprehend those responsible.

Exploration of Serial Killers Who Were Never Caught:

Lastly, our book explores the chilling cases of serial killers who were never caught. These enigmatic individuals continue to elude law enforcement, leaving a trail of unspeakable horror in their wake. By analyzing their crimes and psychological profiles, we hope to bring attention to these unsolved mysteries and inspire renewed efforts to bring these killers to justice.

Conclusion:

In "Fatal Obsessions: A Journey into the Minds of Serial Killers," we provide a comprehensive exploration of the psychological motivations driving these individuals to commit unimaginable acts. Whether you are a true crime enthusiast, criminology student, or simply fascinated by the intricate workings of the human mind, this book offers a gripping and insightful journey into the dark realm of serial killers and their psychological profiles.

The Role of Childhood Trauma in Shaping Serial Killers

In the dark and twisted world of serial killers, there is a common thread that binds many of them together – childhood trauma. This subchapter explores the profound impact of early-life experiences on the minds of these individuals, shedding light on the complex interplay between nature and nurture in the making of a serial killer.

Understanding the Origins:

Serial killers are not born; they are made. While genetics and other factors play a role, childhood trauma often acts as a catalyst, fueling a deadly obsession. By examining the early experiences of notorious serial killers, we can begin to unravel the psychological pathways that lead to such horrifying acts.

Psychological Effects:

Childhood trauma can leave deep emotional scars that shape an individual's perception of the world. Abuse, neglect, and witnessing violence can lead to a range of psychological issues, such as antisocial personality disorder, dissociation, and a distorted sense of self. These mental imprints serve as a breeding ground for the dark fantasies and violent tendencies that later manifest in serial killers.

Unraveling the Trauma:

Exploring the specific traumas experienced by serial killers offers valuable insights. Whether it be the abuse suffered at the hands of a family member, the loss of a loved one, or growing up in a chaotic environment, these experiences influence the development of a disturbed mind. By delving into the details of their past, we can better understand the motivations behind their heinous crimes.

Patterns and Themes:

While each serial killer's story is unique, certain patterns and themes emerge. Female serial killers, for instance, often have a history of childhood sexual abuse, leading to complex issues related to power and control. Serial killers targeting specific demographics, such as children or prostitutes, may have unresolved traumas that drive them to seek dominance over vulnerable individuals.

The Elusive Profiles:

Examining the role of childhood trauma in shaping serial killers' psychological profiles is vital for law enforcement and criminology students. Identifying common characteristics and risk factors can aid in the prevention and detection of future offenders, potentially saving lives and bringing justice to victims.

Conclusion:

The role of childhood trauma in shaping serial killers is a haunting reality that demands our attention. By acknowledging the complex relationship between early-life experiences and criminal behavior, we can gain a deeper understanding of these individuals' motivations and work towards preventing such tragedies in the future. This subchapter serves as a critical resource for true crime enthusiasts, criminology students, and those intrigued by the intricate workings of the human mind.

Psychopathy and Serial Killers: Unraveling the Dark Connection

In the world of true crime, few topics captivate our imagination like the chilling realm of serial killers. These individuals, driven by their dark desires, commit heinous acts that baffle and terrify us. But what lies beneath the surface of their disturbed minds? This subchapter delves into the intricate relationship between psychopathy and serial killers, offering a glimpse into the twisted psyche that drives these monsters.

Understanding Psychopathy:

To comprehend the connection between psychopathy and serial killers, we must first understand the nature of psychopathy itself. Defined by a lack of empathy, remorse, and a penchant for manipulation, psychopathy is a personality disorder that lies at the heart of many notorious serial killers. Through an exploration of their psychological profiles, we uncover the common traits and behaviors exhibited by those who commit these horrific crimes.

The Psychopathic Serial Killer:

Drawing from real-life cases and psychological studies, we dissect the mind of a psychopathic serial killer. We examine their modus operandi, whether they are stranglers, poisoners, or have other distinct methods of killing. Additionally, we explore the chilling phenomenon of serial killers targeting specific demographics, such as children or prostitutes, shedding light on the motivations and distorted fantasies that drive their actions.

Unsolved Serial Killings:

While some serial killers are apprehended and brought to justice, others remain elusive, leaving behind a trail of unsolved mysteries. This subchapter investigates the psychological complexities of serial killers who were never caught, unraveling the reasons behind their ability to evade law enforcement and continue their reign of terror.

Psychopathy and Regional Patterns:

Serial killers are not limited by borders, and their activities have been documented across various regions and countries. We delve into the intriguing connection between psychopathy and regional patterns, examining how cultural, environmental, and societal factors shape the development of serial killers in different parts of the world.

Conclusion:

In this subchapter, we have embarked on a journey

into the minds of serial killers, guided by the dark thread of psychopathy that connects them. By understanding the psychological underpinnings of these individuals, we gain valuable insights into their motivations, their methods, and the terrifying world they inhabit. Whether you are a true crime enthusiast, a criminology student, or simply fascinated by the complex psychology of serial killers, this exploration into the dark connection between psychopathy and their actions will leave you with a deeper understanding of these chilling individuals.

Chapter 9

Conclusion

The Importance of Combating Serial Killers and Protecting Society: A Comprehensive Perspective

Serial killers, with their gruesome crimes and intricate psychological profiles, have carved a dark niche in the annals of true crime. In "Fatal Obsessions: A Journey into the Minds of Serial Killers," we delve deep into the twisted psyches of these individuals, unraveling their motives, methods, and the profound impact they have on society. This subchapter aims to offer a comprehensive perspective on the vital importance of combating serial killers and safeguarding our communities from their heinous acts.

Understanding Behavioral Patterns and Warning Signs:

Studying serial killers provides a unique opportunity to grasp the behavioral patterns and warning signs that precede their violent acts. By meticulously examining their psychological profiles, investigators can identify commonalities and early indicators that may signal someone's descent into the realm of serial killing. This knowledge becomes a powerful tool in preventing future atrocities, allowing authorities to intervene before more lives are tragically cut short.

Targeted Preventative Measures for Vulnerable Populations:

Serial killers often exhibit a disturbing pattern of targeting specific demographics, such as children, prostitutes, or individuals from particular regions. Understanding these patterns enables law enforcement agencies and communities to implement targeted preventative measures. By focusing resources on vulnerable populations and heightening awareness within these communities, we create a more resilient defense against those who prey on the most susceptible members of society.

Solving Unsolved Cases for Community Healing:

Unsolved serial killings cast a long shadow over

communities, fostering fear and uncertainty. By dedicating efforts to examining these cold cases, we aim to reignite public interest and potentially uncover new leads or information. Solving these unsolved mysteries not only brings justice but also provides a sense of closure and security to the affected communities. It is a testament to the commitment of law enforcement and the resilience of communities that refuse to let these cases fade into obscurity.

Understanding Modus Operandi for Effective Investigation:

The diversity within the realm of serial killers extends to their chosen methods—be it strangulation, poisoning, or other distinctive approaches. Understanding the intricacies of their modus operandi allows law enforcement agencies to develop effective investigative techniques and strategies. Recognizing the distinct characteristics of each killer's method empowers authorities to make connections between seemingly unrelated cases, facilitating the identification and apprehension of these predators.

Our Responsibility to Protect Society:

The overarching importance of combating serial killers lies in our collective responsibility to protect society. By unraveling the psychology, motives, and methods of these individuals, we can develop proactive measures to prevent future tragedies. "Fatal Obsessions" aims to provide a comprehensive exploration of serial killers, empowering true crime enthusiasts, criminology students, and those interested in the subject matter to contribute actively to the fight against these predators. Together, we can strive for a safer, more secure society, free from the terror imposed by these malevolent figures.

In conclusion, the battle against serial killers is multifaceted, encompassing understanding, prevention, and resolution. "Fatal Obsessions" invites readers to join the quest for justice and security, acknowledging the collective responsibility we bear to protect our communities from the chilling menace of serial killers.

Appendix

Glossary of Terms

In the dark and twisted world of serial killers, understanding the vocabulary surrounding these crimes is crucial. Whether you are a true crime enthusiast, a criminology student, or simply someone intrigued by the minds of these cold-blooded murderers, this glossary of terms will provide you with a comprehensive understanding of the language associated with serial killers.

1. Serial Killer: A person who commits a series of murders, typically targeting multiple victims over a period of time, with a cooling-off period between each crime.

2. Modus Operandi: The specific method or pattern used by a serial killer to commit their crimes. This can include strangulation, poisoning, dismemberment, or other distinct patterns that differentiate one killer from another.

3. Signature: The unique and often ritualistic behavior or characteristic left by a serial killer at the crime scene. This can serve as a calling card or a way for the killer to assert control over their victims.

4. Victimology: The study of the demographic characteristics of serial killers' victims. This includes factors such as age, gender, occupation, and lifestyle choices that may make certain individuals more vulnerable to becoming targets.

5. Profiling: The process of creating a psychological profile of a serial killer based on their crime scenes, behavior, and other evidence. This helps law enforcement agencies understand the motivations, patterns, and characteristics of the killer in order to aid in their capture.

6. Unsolved Serial Killings: Cases in which a serial killer remains unidentified or at large, leaving law enforcement agencies and the public with unanswered questions and ongoing fear.

7. Female Serial Killers: A term used to describe women who commit multiple murders. Female serial killers often employ different methods and motivations compared to their male counterparts.

8. Geographic Profiling: The analysis of the locations and patterns of a serial killer's crimes to help identify their possible residence or areas of familiarity. This technique can be a valuable tool in narrowing down suspects and focusing investigative efforts.

9. Psychopathy: A personality disorder characterized by a lack of empathy, remorse, and a propensity for manipulative and antisocial behavior. Many serial killers exhibit psychopathic traits, making it an important aspect of their psychological profile.

10. Media Frenzy: The intense public interest and media coverage that surrounds high-profile serial killer cases. This can often lead to sensationalism and distortion of the facts, causing further fear and fascination among the general public.

As you delve into the pages of "Fatal Obsessions: A Journey into the Minds of Serial Killers," this glossary will serve as your guide through the intricate language and concepts surrounding these chilling crimes. With each term, you will gain a deeper understanding of the psychological complexities and motivations that drive these killers to commit their heinous acts. Whether you are studying criminology or simply seeking a spine-chilling read, this glossary will provide you with the essential knowledge to navigate the dark depths of the world's most notorious serial killers.

List of Infamous Serial Killers

In the dark underbelly of humanity, certain individuals have left a chilling mark on history through their heinous acts of violence. This subchapter, titled "List of Infamous Serial Killers," aims to provide a comprehensive overview of some of the most notorious and fascinating serial killers the world has ever known. From their horrifying crimes to their psychological profiles, this list will captivate the attention of true crime enthusiasts and criminology students alike.

1. Ted Bundy: Known for his charm and charisma, Bundy was a master manipulator who preyed on young women, often luring them to their deaths. His story offers insights into the psychology of a serial killer and the dangers of underestimating their ability to blend into society.

2. Aileen Wuornos: One of the few female serial killers, Wuornos targeted and killed several men she claimed had assaulted or attempted to assault her. Her troubled upbringing and traumatic experiences shed light on the complex relationship between nature and nurture in the formation of a serial killer.

3. Jack the Ripper: Perhaps the most infamous unidentified serial killer of all time, Jack the Ripper terrorized the streets of London in the late 1800s, targeting prostitutes. The unsolved nature of his crimes continues to captivate the minds of true crime enthusiasts, sparking countless theories and debates.

4. John Wayne Gacy: Operating in the 1970s, Gacy disguised himself as a friendly neighborhood clown while secretly murdering young boys and burying

them beneath his own home. The contrast between his public persona and his sinister actions showcases the chilling duality often present in serial killers.

5. The Yorkshire Ripper: Peter Sutcliffe's reign of terror in Northern England during the late 1970s and early 1980s left the nation gripped with fear. Targeting mainly prostitutes, Sutcliffe's case raises questions about society's responsibility to protect vulnerable demographics.

6. The Boston Strangler: This unidentified serial killer struck fear into the hearts of Boston residents in the early 1960s. Targeting women, the Strangler's crimes highlighted the vulnerability of individuals within their own homes and the importance of community awareness.

7. The Zodiac Killer: Operating in Northern California during the late 1960s and early 1970s, the Zodiac Killer taunted the public and law enforcement alike with cryptic messages. Despite numerous suspects, the killer's true identity remains unknown, leaving behind a legacy of unsolved mystery.

Each of these infamous serial killers offers a unique glimpse into the dark recesses of the human mind. By exploring their crimes and analyzing their psychological profiles, "Fatal Obsessions: A Journey into the Minds of Serial Killers" provides a captivating and chilling journey into the world of these twisted individuals. Whether you are a true crime enthusiast, a criminology student, or simply intrigued by the complexities of the human psyche, this list will both intrigue and disturb, leaving you with a deeper understanding of the chilling world of serial killers.

Recommended Further Reading

For those who have been captivated by the chilling accounts of serial killers in "Fatal Obsessions: A Journey into the Minds of Serial Killers," there is no doubt that the fascination with these dark individuals will continue. If you are a true crime enthusiast or a criminology student eager to delve deeper into the minds of these murderers, we have compiled a list of recommended further reading for you. These books will provide you with more in-depth knowledge about serial killers, their motives, their methods, and the psychological profiles that drive them.

1. "Mindhunter: Inside the FBI's Elite Serial Crime Unit" by John E. Douglas and Mark Olshaker: Dive into the world of criminal profiling with this gripping memoir by FBI profiler John E. Douglas. Learn about the development of the Behavioral Science Unit and gain insight into the minds of notorious killers like Ted Bundy and Charles Manson.

2. "The Stranger Beside Me" by Ann Rule: Ann Rule,

a former police officer-turned-true crime writer, tells the shocking story of her personal relationship with one of the most infamous serial killers, Ted Bundy. This book offers a unique perspective on Bundy's double life and the struggles of coming to terms with the truth.

3. "Female Serial Killers: How and Why Women Become Monsters" by Peter Vronsky: Explore the often overlooked world of female serial killers with this comprehensive study by true crime expert Peter Vronsky. Uncover the motivations and psychological factors that drive women to commit heinous crimes.

4. "Zodiac" by Robert Graysmith: Delve into one of the most perplexing unsolved serial killings in American history. Graysmith meticulously documents the chilling crimes of the Zodiac Killer and the subsequent investigation, offering a fascinating glimpse into the mind of an elusive murderer.

5. "The Serial Killer Files: The Who, What, Where, How, and Why of the World's Most Terrifying Murderers" by Harold Schechter: This comprehensive guide provides a detailed overview of serial killers throughout history. From infamous figures like Jack the Ripper to lesser-known killers, Schechter offers a captivating examination of their crimes and the psychological factors that contribute to their actions.

Whether you are interested in specific types of serial killers, unsolved cases, or the psychological profiles of these murderers, these recommended readings will satisfy your curiosity. Remember, these books offer a deeper understanding of the darkest corners of the human psyche, allowing you to explore the minds of these killers while maintaining a safe distance. Happy reading, and may these insights contribute to your knowledge of the true crime world.

Resources for Criminology Students and True Crime Enthusiasts

In this subchapter, we will explore a comprehensive list of resources that cater to the interests of both criminology students and true crime enthusiasts. Whether you are fascinated by the twisted minds of serial killers, interested in the psychology behind their crimes, or intrigued by unsolved mysteries, this collection of resources will provide you with a wealth of information and further deepen your understanding of this dark and complex field.

1. Books: "Fatal Obsessions: A Journey into the Minds of Serial Killers" by Morgan B Jeffery - This book, which forms the basis of our discussion, offers an in-depth exploration of the psychological profiles of serial killers, their motives, and their methods.

2. Websites and Online Forums: Explore websites

dedicated to true crime, such as CrimeLibrary.com, which provides extensive case studies, profiles of infamous serial killers, and articles on various aspects of criminology. Online forums like Reddit's r/TrueCrime offer a platform for discussions and sharing insights with fellow enthusiasts.

3. Documentaries and Podcasts: Delve into the world of true crime through gripping documentaries and podcasts. Netflix's "Mindhunter" and "The Confession Tapes" offer compelling insights into the minds of serial killers. Popular true crime podcasts like "Sword and Scale" and "My Favorite Murder" provide in-depth discussions on fascinating cases.

4. Academic Journals and Research Papers: For criminology students seeking more specialized information, academic journals such as the Journal of Investigative Psychology and Offender Profiling provide in-depth research on topics like the modus operandi of serial killers, psychological theories, and case studies.

5. Forensic Science Resources: Understanding the role of forensic science is crucial in the study of serial killers. Books like "Forensic Science: An Introduction" by Richard Saferstein and websites like ForensicMag.com offer valuable insights into forensic techniques used in criminal investigations.

6. Podcasts and Books on Unsolved Serial Killings: For those intrigued by unsolved cases, podcasts like "The Trail Went Cold" and books like "The Encyclopedia of Unsolved Crimes" by Michael Newton delve into fascinating mysteries that continue to baffle investigators.

7. True Crime Documentaries and TV Shows: Expand your knowledge through gripping true crime documentaries like "The Ted Bundy Tapes" and TV shows like "Criminal Minds," which provide fictional but insightful portrayals of serial killers and their psychology.

8. Online Libraries and Databases: Access online resources such as JSTOR, ProQuest, and Google Scholar to find academic papers, dissertations, and research articles that explore various aspects of criminology, including specific demographics targeted by serial killers or their operational regions.

By utilizing these resources, both criminology students and true crime enthusiasts can gain a deeper understanding of serial killers, their psychological profiles, and the various aspects of criminology that surround their crimes. Whether you are interested in infamous cases, unsolved mysteries, or the intricacies of forensic science, these resources will provide you with a solid foundation to further explore the fascinating world of true crime.

www.ingramcontent.com/pod-product-compliance
Lightning Source LLC
Chambersburg PA
CBHW071358130726
47996CB00002B/987